# Animal Homes

Jennifer Bové

muddy boots™

we jump in puddles

Guilford, Connecticut

Published by Muddy Boots
An imprint of Globe Pequot
MuddyBootsBooks.com

Distributed by NATIONAL BOOK NETWORK

Book design by Katie Jennings Design

Front cover photo © Getty Images/Missing35mm, back cover photo © Getty Images/Piero Malaer, title page and page 17 © Getty Images/Ken Canning, table of contents and page 12 © Getty Images/Bart van den Dikkenberg, page 2 © Getty Images/Kenneth Canning, page 5 © Getty Images/Dieter Meyrl, page 6 © Getty Images/Daniel Cox, page 8 © iStock/Shumba138, page 9 © Getty Images/Holger Mette, page 11 © Getty Images/Savushkin, page 13 © Getty Images/Bucky_za, page 14 © Getty Images/Tirc83, page 16 © Getty Images/Danita Delimont, page 18 © Getty Images/Brian E. Kushner, page 19 © Getty Images/Sharon Paris, page 20 © Getty Images/Georgette Douwma, page 22 © Getty Images/Paul Souders, page 24 © Getty Images/Comstock Images, page 26 © Getty Images/MisterSandman, page 27 © Hans Lelijnsa/NiS/Minden Pictures, page 28 © Getty Images/hardeko, page 29 © Getty Images/Robert McGouey.

The National Wildlife Federation & Ranger Rick contributors: Children's Publication Staff, Licensing Staff including Deana Duffek, Michael Morris & Kristen Ferriere, and the National Wildlife Federation in-house naturalist David Mizejewski

Thank you for joining the National Wildlife Federation and Muddy Boots in preserving endangered animals and protecting vital wildlife habits. The National Wildlife is a voice for wildlife protection, dedicated to preserving America's outdoor traditions and inspiring generations of conservationists.

British Library Cataloguing-in-Publication Information available

Library of Congress Control Number: 2016912766

ISBN 978-1-63076-224-7 (paperback)
ISBN 978-1-63076-225-4 (electronic)

™ The paper used in this publication meets the minimum requirements of American National Standard for Information Sciences—Permanence of Paper for Printed Library Materials, ANSI/NISO Z39.48-1992.

Printed in the United States of America

# Contents

Knock, knock!
Is anybody home?
Animals live in all
kinds of houses.

These raccoons are peeking out from their home in a tree.

## DENS

A mother grizzly bear and her cub live in a hole under rocks. Their home is called a den.

Red fox
kits come
out of their
den to play.

Weaverbirds weave their homes out of grass. This type of home is called a nest.

A wasp
builds a nest
with many
rooms for
its babies.

Meerkats pop up to take a look outside their underground home. Their home is called a burrow.

This burrowing owl sits beside the entrance to its burrow.

A red-bellied woodpecker makes its nest in a hole in a tree.

Great horned owl chicks are at home in these old trees, too.

A hermit crab
lives in a shell.
It takes the
shell wherever
it goes.

A tortoise is another animal that carries its home on its back.

This moray eel makes its home in a coral reef under the sea.

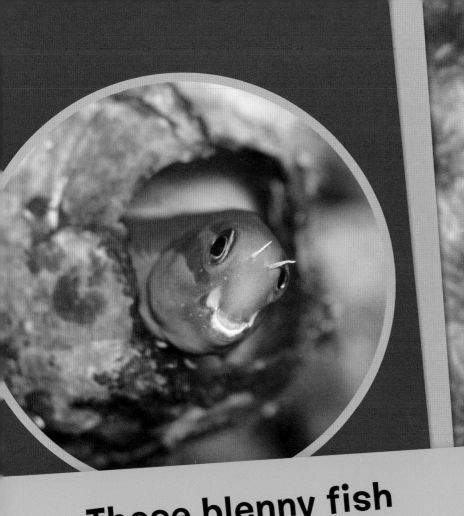

These blenny fish peek out from their home in a coral reef.

A beaver builds a home in a pond with sticks and mud. A beaver's home is called a lodge.

**Author:** JENNIFER BOVÉ

**Question:** If you were an animal, what would be your favorite kind of home?

**Answer:** My favorite animal home would be a nest in a tree. It would be fun to build a nest and live up in the forest canopy like a weaverbird.

**National Wildlife Federation Naturalist:** DAVID MIZEJEWSKI

**Question:** What's the most amazing animal home you've ever seen?

**Answer:** I think the tunnels that gopher tortoises dig are amazing. They can be 10 feet deep and 40 feet long, and over 400 other wildlife species from owls to frogs to mice rely on them for shelter.

**Illustrator:** PARKER JACOBS *(Ranger Rick & Ricky characters)*

**Question:** Where in your home is your favorite place to draw?

**Answer:** In my home, I like to draw on the living room couch. That's where I'm very comfortable and can get great ideas of what to draw by looking out the window and viewing nature, or by seeing my family do silly things.